YOUR
DAILY
HOROSCOPE

✹

YOUR
DAILY
HOROSCOPE

✺

NIK DE DOMINIC

NEW MICHIGAN PRESS
TUCSON, ARIZONA

NEW MICHIGAN PRESS
DEPT OF ENGLISH, P. O. BOX 210067
UNIVERSITY OF ARIZONA
TUCSON, AZ 85721-0067

<http://newmichiganpress.com>

Orders and queries to nmp@thediagram.com.

Copyright © 2015 by Nik De Dominic.
All rights reserved.

ISBN 978-1-934832-51-6. FIRST PRINTING.

Printed in the United States of America.

Design by Ander Monson.

Cover image © Sasidis | Dreamstime.com — Empty Seats Photo

CONTENTS

Your Daily Horoscope *[Twenty years ago…]*   1
Your Daily Horoscope *[Someone shares a picture…]*   2
Your Daily Horoscope *[You have a moon…]*   4
Your Daily Horoscope *[On the Chinatown bus…]*   5
Your Daily Horoscope *[Someone will send…]*   7
Your Daily Horoscope *[Someone will share…]*   8
Your Daily Horoscope *[Fall is finally here…]*   9
Your Daily Horoscope *[The Chinatown bus…]*   10
Your Daily Horoscope *[Well, Stargazer, today…]*   11
Your Daily Horoscope *[Today, Stargazer…]*   12
Your Daily Horoscope *[Dr. John sang…]*   13
Your Daily Horoscope *[You build…]*   14
Your Daily Horoscope *[In the sawdust...]*   15
Your Daily Horoscope *[The men take…]*   16
Your Daily Horoscope *[You will wake…]*   17
Your Daily Horoscope *[You will get…]*   18
Your Daily Horoscope *[The Chinatown bus…]*   20
Your Daily Horoscope *[There is a beach…]*   21
Your Daily Horoscope *[The Mayans called…]*   23
How Long Can Your Sign Hold a Grudge   24
A Note for Reading Your Daily Horoscopes   25

Acknowledgments   29

YOUR DAILY HOROSCOPE

Twenty years ago Dizzy had some racket with Impalas
and could have keys cut to VIN numbers. A perfumed
icon hanging from the rear view as we drove around
doing crimes. Now I ride the 794 to work and I think
Dizzy is dead. Everyone on this line is infirmed somehow,
walkers and wheelchairs, boils and bald, reeks of salad dressing, and I
am trying to figure out what my problem is. Big and beautiful
blonde boys bring their bibles on the bus, sit closely
together in starched white short shirt sleeves, murmur to each other
secrets of the after this. Is it a bible, the thing Mormons morm from?
The strip-mall church off San Fernando, Pentecostal something or other,
is giving away food and there is a line out the door,
up both sides of the block. A little girl with black bangs hangs
in her parents' hands over a pack of pigeons, brethren grieving
over a fallen and headless brother, and she spits at them to scatter.
When I get home still afternoon we lie in bed and let the house go
from day to blue. I tell you I read today that you are everyone
in your dreams. No shit, you say, who else would you be?

YOUR DAILY HOROSCOPE

Someone shares a picture of all the astrological signs
followed by this: The stars and planets will not affect

your life in anyway. It's true. *The Voice* is on at 7
and I'm eating nachos. We have a trainer

for our dog because it is "leash aggressive."
This is not entirely true:

It's just fucking aggressive.
A Katrina dog, street puppy.

Today on the internet someone shares
Tinder for dogs: It's like real life but better.

Single white corgi mix seeks same for
no strings attached fun (must be fixed).

Long, silent stares across blocks, sleeping
on dirty laundry. Some intimacy issues.

Someone shares one of the guys from *Car Talk* died today
and a young girl with terminal cancer killed herself.

The Brazilian student-teacher sex-tape is a hoax,
not a student and not a teacher. An attractive man

in Santa Cruz beat a man with an umbrella
for wearing a Fox News costume on Halloween

and the internet has a new sexiest mug-shot contender,
soon his face photo-shopped into Givenchy ads.

The stars and planets will not affect
your life in anyway. None of this will.

YOUR DAILY HOROSCOPE

You have a moon in your second house,
Stargazer, and he's a terrible tenant.
Slovenly he doesn't work, watches
Ellen all day, slightly shimmying when she dances,
sits on the porch in the afternoon and leers
at the neighborhood kids on their Huffies in a way
that makes no one comfortable. Cocaine-fueled parties
every night, broken porcelain toilets and tubs.
The moon was moving through some financial problems
when he signed the lease so out of the kindness of your heart
you forewent deposit. You don't even have that recourse.
You've called the county but eviction
is a slow moving process in Star City.

YOUR DAILY HOROSCOPE

On the Chinatown bus a woman will witness you.
I prayed to Jesus for girls and they kept coming:
Tony and Dennis and Tyler and Troy and Reggie.

You don't question this. A man next to you will study
a manila folder full of xeroxes of handwritten notes.
Childlike scrawl, every letter drawn over and over itself

so that Ys look like trees stricken by cat's claw and wisteria
reminding you of the south you left. There is a crude circle cut
in triangles, each an astrological sign: the sign under which

Christ was born and Abraham too. Simple reckoning in the
    marginalia, the constant
mention of the Mayans, their calendar. A note: my heart is
    broken in 3 halves.
When films were made and under which moon, *The Wizard
    of Oz* (1939).

You would ask questions if you this weren't a stranger, you not
    on the bus reading
over his shoulder. A child will fall into your lap at an abrupt
    stop. Your stop.
At the corner Jehovah's Witnesses will hand out pamphlets—
    Is Satan Real?

A kid with a diamond tipped scribe will etch his name
in the storefront glass
of the mostly costume jewelry shop until the owner
bangs on the window.
Make your way to work, say hello to Sabrina, Google
the Scarecrow, him torn apart.

YOUR DAILY HOROSCOPE

Someone will send you a .gif
of a clown tying a noose
around his neck to a sapling.
He will then water the sapling.
Everywhere a .gif a gift.

YOUR DAILY HOROSCOPE

Someone will share an article
about a dog's gaze, why we bond
with it like a child. Rover's look
releases oxytocin. The cuddle chemical
encourages bonding between
mothers and offspring
and is also responsible for coupling.
Someone else will ask
what happens if the dog's blind.
People are dicks.

YOUR DAILY HOROSCOPE

Fall is finally here. Leaves
leafing and everywhere a pumpkin
spice. Did you know there's no pumpkin
in pumpkin spice? I want you to think
about that today, Stargazer. And imagine
the latte. You are the latte. No, not foamy
and overpriced. But deceptive in your flavoring.
You may taste like one thing but you are
a different thing entirely. In this case, high-fructose
corn syrup. But that's neither here nor there.
Also, this—the latte exists in concentrate.
There is very little liquid milk there
before it's foamed and takes its shape.
There's something there, a science lesson
for you: something about volume
and density and space. I'd tell you more
but that's for you to decipher this day
and I went to poetry school.

YOUR DAILY HOROSCOPE

The Chinatown bus is unusually crowded today.
You move your way to the back and stand
between two women catching up. From conversation
it is evident they have not seen each other
for a long time. That maybe they used to work
together: The blonde guy with acne,
dead. Terry? Dead, too. And the guy
that looked like a weasel. He disappeared.
No one has seen him. You begin to wonder
if they are cops but you know cops don't take the bus.
When your father sold Fords he told you
cops had the worst credit. It isn't until
they begin to discuss Katey Sagal
and her evolution as an actress since *Married with Children*
that you realize they are talking about not work
but *Sons of Anarchy*. When you get home that night,
take off all of your clothes, turn off the lights
and wait for your lover. When your lover comes
through the door, tell your lover you want to taste his glands.

YOUR DAILY HOROSCOPE

Well, Stargazer, today is your day.
Kind of. Imagine you just moved to a new region
and for the last six months you'd been applying
for jobs. Today every resume you sent in
will be returned. All 8,000 of them.
When one call is done, the phone will ring.
You pick it up, call waiting interrupts.
You get a notification on Facebook, then another.
Your Instagram photograph of a dog in a tie has 1,000
    new likes.
Cute picture, one writes. Want to come work for us?
Your email pings. And then again. And again.
They begin to sense your fraying
and like teenage lovers become incensed:
what, you don't want to work for us? Well, fine.
No, that's not what I mean, hold on, one second,
you say. The comments become angry.
Soon they are all at your front door,
pitchforks, torches, gnawing at each other,
throwing out offers, benefits, matching 401ks.
Before the riot, you shutter the windows,
put your phone into airplane mode and go
back to bed. The covers are cool to the touch,
and you dream of riding an endless escalator endlessly.

YOUR DAILY HOROSCOPE

Today, Stargazer,
unfortunately, everything
will break. Horoscope,
from the Latin, literally,
time observer. You are
the watcher. Today,
Stargazer, time will
break. So will teeth
and bone and nail.
Infrastructures will
crumble. Blood
in the streets.
The dogs will yowl.
First, meteors, then fire,
then as they say, all hell
will break loose.

        This is all ok, Stargazer.
Reading your charts,
I can say this would be a good time
to take personal inventory and decide
what it is most important to you
so that you may stockpile it in
your survivalist uncle's bunker
in the desert off I-90.
Bring those peanut butter cookies I like.
The ones from Trader Joe's.

YOUR DAILY HOROSCOPE

Dr. John sang, *Your steak ain't no hipper than my pork chop,
your Cadillac no hipper than my bus stop, your champagne no
 hipper*

than my soda pop. I don't know if I agree with him
unless he cooks a really good pork chop, sure,

but really, champagne and soda isn't a useful comparison.
They are totally different things—one's got booze in it—and
 Dr. John

is ugly as fuck. What I do want you to take from this,
 Stargazer, is I was born
in the #12 St. Louis cemetery at midnight in New Orleans
 birthed by 12 midwives

to 12 fathers in a litter of 12. No one cried, no one
 celebrated. The moon and 12 stars
pricked my eyes open early, all the other kittens staying
 dumb and blind another 12 weeks.

My kin were all picked off by a 12 pack of opossum and I
 was the first to catch a sparrow
in my mouth to leave 12 feathers on your pillow and I won't
 stop until another 12 I get.

YOUR DAILY HOROSCOPE

You build
to build
to build
a door
to a door
stairway to
stairway
how do
you enter
a place
with no
beginning
and con-
structed
without end
a closet opens
to a closet
inside a
small box
full of boxes:
a feather
a tooth
a shotgun shell
a fingernail.

YOUR DAILY HOROSCOPE

In the sawdust the children dance.
The children dance in the sawdust.

In red hood holding your sleeve,
you walk towards a man, your shadow.

Your feet kick up this dust. This earth
in shade clouds around.

In this field we will find each other.
We will find each other in this field.

YOUR DAILY HOROSCOPE

The men take us in the forest they come upon our tents in the night and take us sleeping from slumber in our sleep the men take us in the forest they come through the woods leaves under toes crushing and they take us sleeping from our slumber while we sleep the men take us trampling the ground with their feet they put their hands to our necks and take us from our sleeping forest in our tents the men take us they are covered in mud smeared on their faces across our faces the men take us in the forest when we sleep in our slumber and we keep close and tight in the night our back to one another's as we sleep one of us always watchful with an eye toward the horizon we see the men coming to take us in the forest and there is not a damn thing anyone can do as the sun sets and someone nods off and the guard is lost to the night the men take us in the forest when they come upon our tents in the night putting their hands to our mouths the mud on the breath the glint of their knives in their eyes to our necks the men take us in the forest while we sleep in our slumber peacefully waiting always waiting for the men.

YOUR DAILY HOROSCOPE

You will wake up today with a fifteen year old song in your head in a terrible OCD kind of way. When you shower, you will ceaselessly hum, your mouth full of toothbrush and pop notes, you will froth toothpaste all over your pubic hair. Walking the dog, on the bus, in the office, you won't shake it. You will doodle lyric on a company pad while making telemarketing calls to people you imagine in ren-faire biz casual—billowy skirts, riding boots, and transition lenses that no longer transition, stuck somewhere between baseball game and bedtime—so that they can renew their database subscriptions. After a particularly bad interaction with a CEO's gatekeeper, it will happen, you will say: *I'm sorry, Miss Jackson,* but *I am for real. Thank you for your time, goodbye.* Later in the bathroom, while urinating, you will look at your genitals and apologize a million more times.

YOUR DAILY HOROSCOPE

You will get a note
that someone
important
died.
You will not
be able to place
the name
or relationship.
You will wake
up in a dream
where all your friends
are grieving.
They will all talk
in fake southern accents
and wear
phony black moustaches.
Even the women
like vaudevillian villains
and they will pretend
not to know you.
And you will say,
but it's me, it's me.
They will plan
a train robbery.
And tie you
to the tracks.

They will give you
an in memoriam pamphlet.
Folded in three
over a table
in someone's dim
kitchen light.
and you
will say,
but it's me,
it's me.

YOUR DAILY HOROSCOPE

The Chinatown bus today
is unusually crowded.
The morning is a gun
metal gray and if you
look hard enough you
can see the circular striations
of where the hills were machined.
Everyone is on their cellphones
playing Farmville and Bejeweled,
and no one's volume muted.
The bus is a carnival ride
of self-interest. One guy
literally navel gazes.
You jockey for position
on the upper rail, find
a good spot and open
Facebook. None of the people
you may know you know,
but rather it's tiny pictures
of all the other bus passengers.
When everyone starts singing,
you know all the words.

YOUR DAILY HOROSCOPE

There is a beach. A party. A beach party. You come across this beach party and everyone is in formal wear. Everyone knows your name but you're unable to place theirs. Each face is a soft memory: the inside of a jacket, the backseat of a car, a meal in New Jersey waiting for a train, a shared key bump in a bathroom when you were 19, a class in grad school on *Sir Gawain and the Green Knight*, a street vendor hawking hot tamales in a neighborhood you left years ago. Maybe. You think. But they all know your name. They have read books on making friends and influencing people and they use your name like punctuation, like breathing, like a metronome. Someone suggests lighting a fire but there is no wood, no kindling. You feel immense guilt for not remembering anyone's name and they all knowing yours, and since your clothes are not as a fine, up you offer them. They say thank you and strip you naked. Your underwear, jeans, and shirt lit in a small pile in the sand. They go up quickly in flames and reduce themselves to soft ash in a blue chemical burn. They look to you hungry when there is nothing left, so you give them your skin and fat. It drips, pops and sizzles into the sand, turning to tiny black dots like fossilized sea creatures in the grit. And your fat and skin are enough to cook off and keep them warm as the sun drops below the blanket of sea. Your memories of those attending the party become clearer and you are almost able to place one of them when your bones are tossed into the flame. They say, thank you, father. Do you remember me? They say, thank you, son. Do you remember me? You burn until there is nothing left but sand and sea and stars.

YOUR DAILY HOROSCOPE

The Mayans called,
they want their calendar

back. Some say the stars
are a scam. I sell snakes'

oil and lullabies. I say we
believe whatever we want

to believe. A man will email,
it may be me, saying he's

of distant relation,
that if you give him a dollar

he will return tenfold:
do it this time just to see

what happens. I have faith
in our spectacular possibility.

HOW LONG CAN YOUR SIGN HOLD A GRUDGE

Aries: An avocado to fall from its tree to rest in soil and turn back to soil.

Taurus: The molting of one chickadee and two bull-thrush.

Gemini: A bird in the tree is nothing like two in a tree. Imagine three in your hand.

Cancer: A sapling shipped to Shanghai, cultivated, grown to maturity, harvested, made to paper (+ or − freight logistics).

Leo: The length of time this line requires to root.

Libra: Shorter than above but no longer than below.

Scorpio: There are 18 species of bougainvillea. The time it takes to recite them all.

Sagittarius: You too are an ornamental crawling vine of warm climes.

Capricorn: You have the tail of a fish and head of a goat. If only it were the other way.

Aquarius: To travel to the fifth dimension and back when the moon is in the 7th house.

A NOTE FOR READING YOUR DAILY HOROSCOPES

The preceding horoscopes are intended for purely entertainment purposes. I make no claims, beyond the claims I've made above, about the possible outcome of your life. It is important to remember that the horoscope, like all things, is metaphor, and its application completely subjective—that language, too, is dynamic. Flexible. Destabilized, even. Something about signs and signified, yada, yada (lol, Plato). When I say you sometimes I mean me; when I say I sometimes I mean you. Sometimes when I say we I mean you and I and other times I mean well, it's sort of royal, so I mean me. But other times, I really do mean I and I really do mean you and I really do mean me and I really do mean we. Further, for one stargazer, a new job may mean getting fired. For another, a new job may mean losing an uncle. For yet another, a new job may mean, literally, a new job—like in middle management at a rental car agency. What I will say is this, something good will happen for you soon. I am sure of it. So will something terrible. That, I am also sure.

ACKNOWLEDGMENTS

Thanks to Gillian Hamel, Louise Mathias, and Jessica Piazza for asking for and running earlier versions of several of these poems at *Omniverse*, *Fanzine*, and *Southern Pacific Review*, respectively.

For my poem a day crew—Justin Runge, Carrie Chappell, David Welch, Benjamin Sutton, Avni Janakrai Vyas, Jeremy Allan Hawkins, Michelle Burke, Brett Evans, and S. Whitney Holmes—who read these poems, gave me a place to write them, and let me read their own beautiful work.

The folks at *The Offending Adam*—Andrew Wessels, Cody Todd, Ryan Winet, and S. Whitney Holmes (again)—and those at *New Orleans Review*, namely Mark Yakich and Kristin Sanders; all for being wonderful people to do this thing we do with, doobeedoobeedoo.

Michael Martone, a technician's technician, who taught me you can get a helluva a lot out of one conceit.

And to Janna, a Sagittarian, who's all of the stars, every day.

NIK DE DOMINIC believes in the stars. Work has appeared in *Los Angeles Review, Harpur Palate, Guernica, DIAGRAM*, and elsewhere. He is a founding editor of *The Offending Adam* and a poetry editor of New Orleans Review. He lectures in The Writing Program at the University of Southern California and lives in Los Angeles with his partner Janna and their leash aggressive dog, Dinah.

❈

COLOPHON

Text is set in a digital version of Jenson, designed by Robert Slimbach in 1996, and based on the work of punchcutter, printer, and publisher Nicolas Jenson. The titles are in Futura.

❊

NEW MICHIGAN PRESS, based in Tucson, Arizona, prints poetry and prose chapbooks, especially work that transcends traditional genre. Together with DIAGRAM, NMP sponsors a yearly chapbook competition.

DIAGRAM, a journal of text, art, and schematic, is published bimonthly at THEDIAGRAM.COM. Periodic print anthologies are available from the New Michigan Press at NEWMICHIGANPRESS.COM.

www.ingramcontent.com/pod-product-compliance
Lightning Source LLC
Chambersburg PA
CBHW031508040426
42444CB00007B/1250